Treasures for Two

6 Captivating Duets for
Intermediate to Late Intermediate Pianists

Contents

Foreword

Sharing the musical experience of ensemble playing is one of the most enjoyable rewards of piano study. Friends and family can become a valuable part of a student's musical life by sharing the duets from *Treasures for Two*, Book 2.

These attractive duets encompass a variety of styles and moods, including some ragtime and the blues. Both the primo and secondo parts are written at an equal level of difficulty.

So find a duet partner, and let the music from *Treasures for Two*, Book 2, add variety and fun to your musical experiences!

Music engraving: Nancy Butler
Cover art: © A. Bryant/Stockworks
Cover design: Candace Smith/Ted Engelbart

Martha Mier

Blueberry Rag
Secondo

Martha Mier

Blueberry Rag

Primo

Moderately (Play ♫ evenly)

Martha Mier

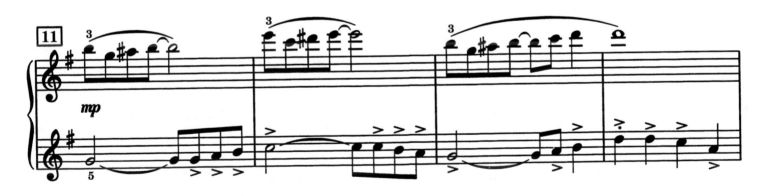

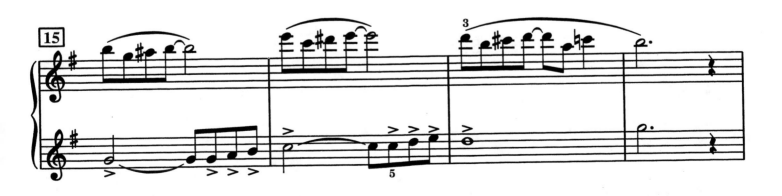

Secondo

Primo

Moonbeams
Secondo

Unhurried, smoothly

Martha Mier

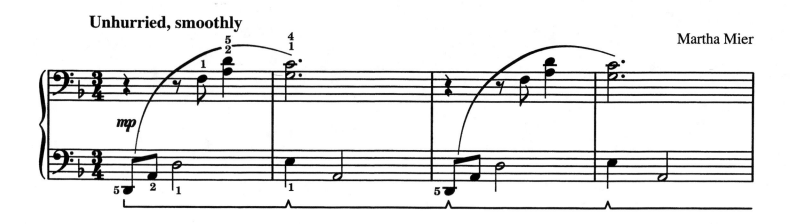

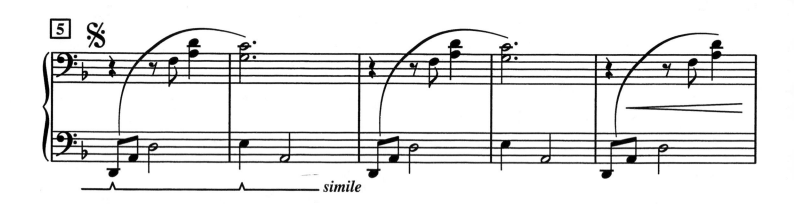

Moonbeams
Primo

Martha Mier

Secondo

Primo

Happy-Go-Lucky

Secondo

Martha Mier

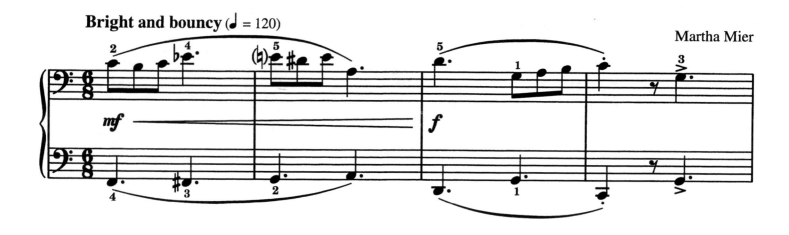

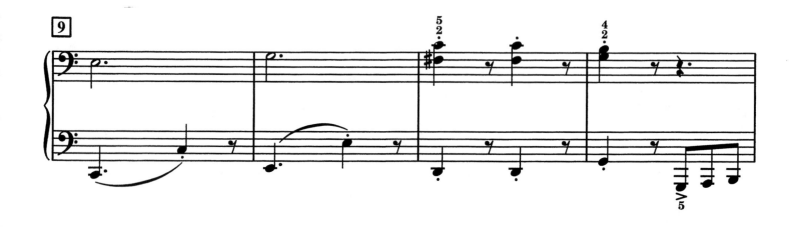

Happy-Go-Lucky

Primo

Martha Mier

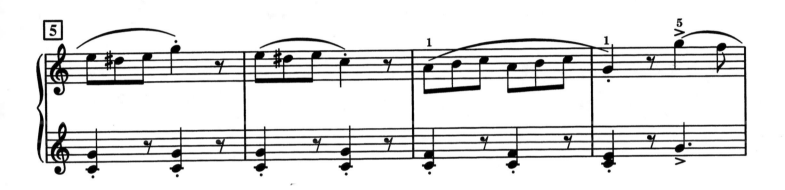

Secondo

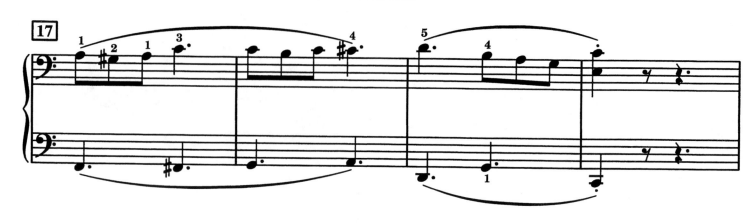

Primo

Secondo

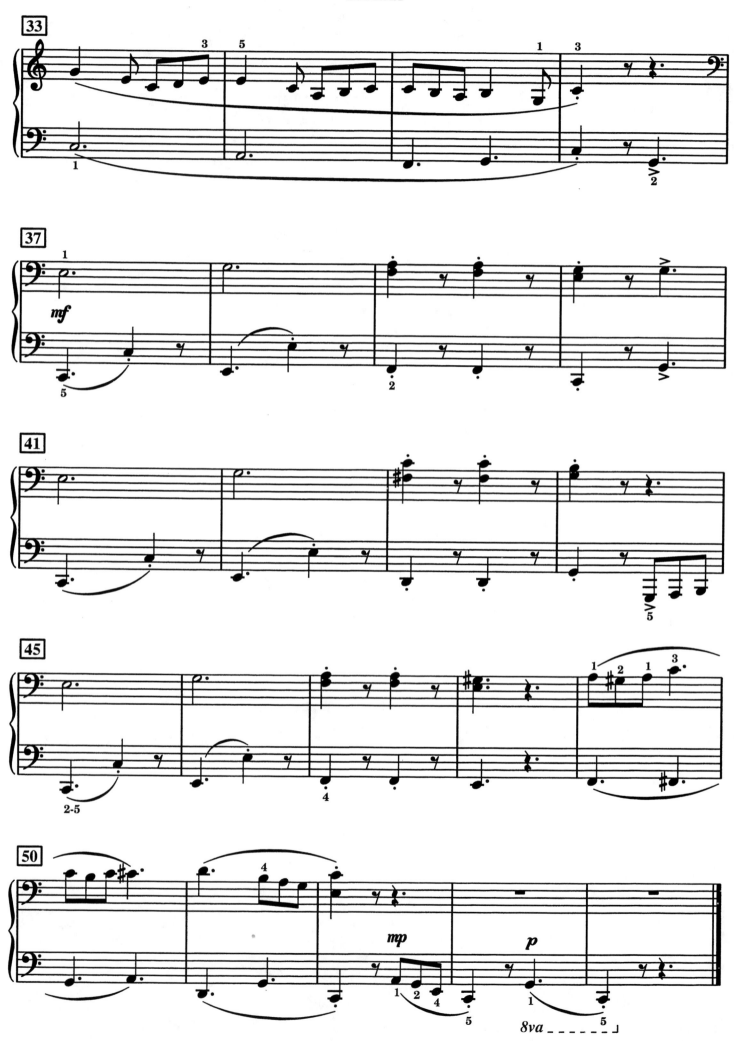

Primo

Biloxi Blues

Secondo

Slow blues swing (♩ = 66)

Martha Mier

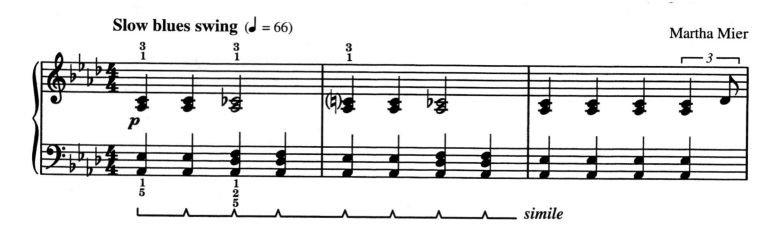

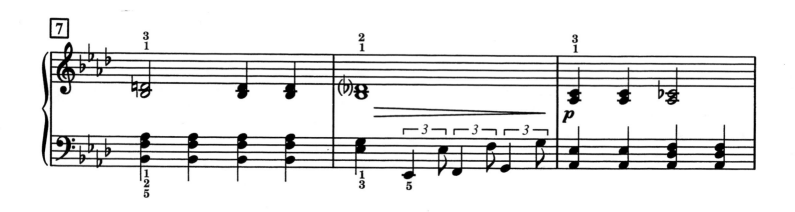

Biloxi Blues

Primo

Martha Mier

Secondo

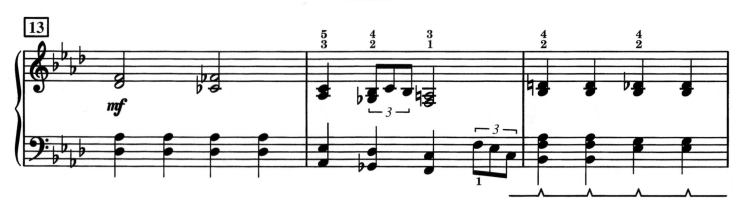

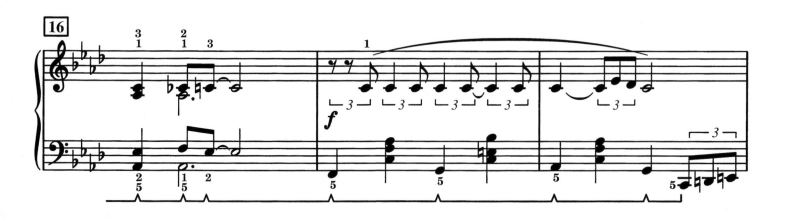

Primo

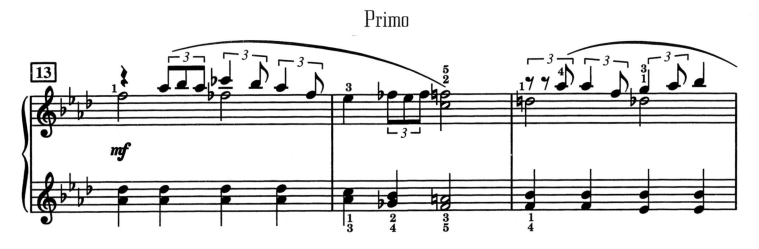

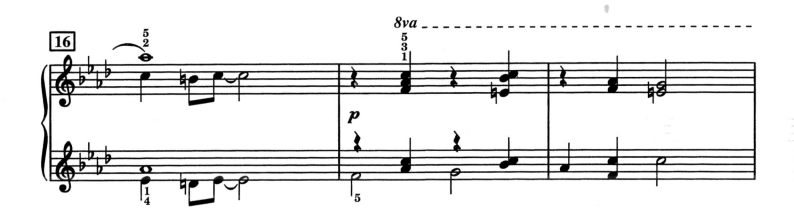

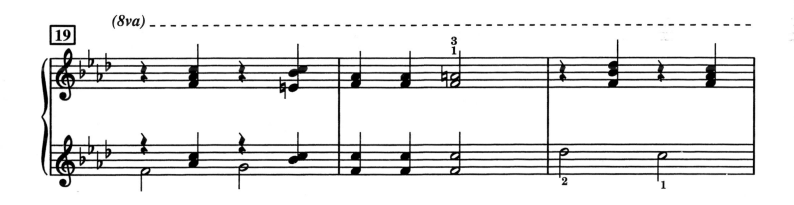

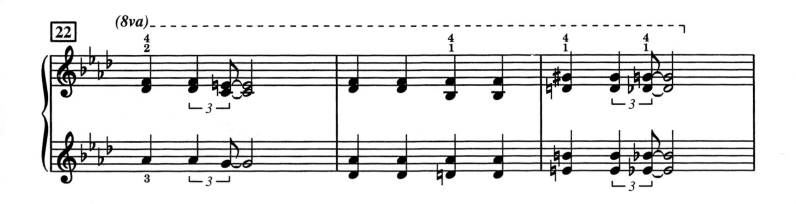

Secondo

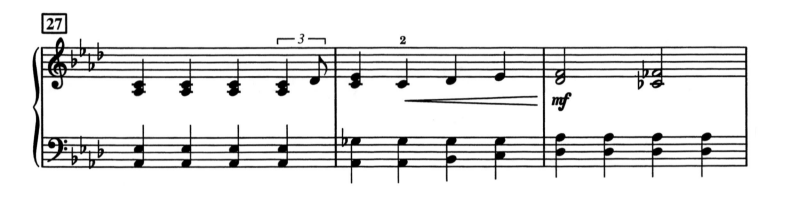

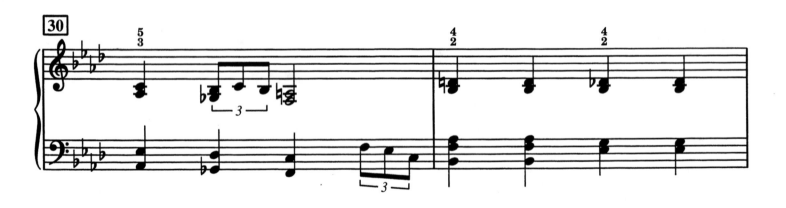

Primo

Western Plains

Secondo

Martha Mier

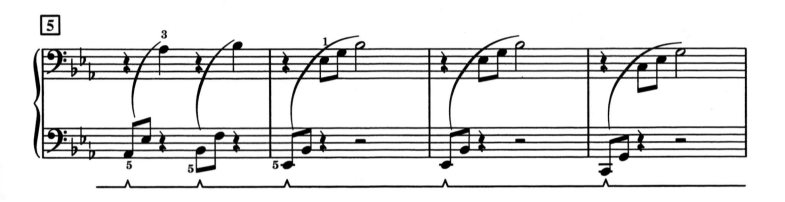

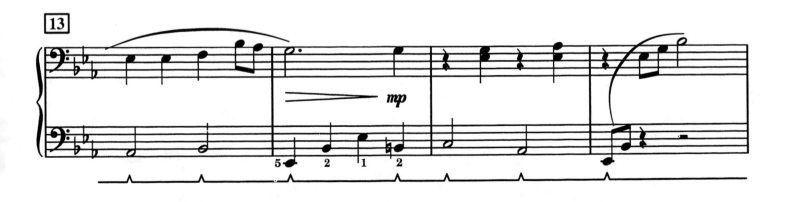

Western Plains

Primo

Martha Mier

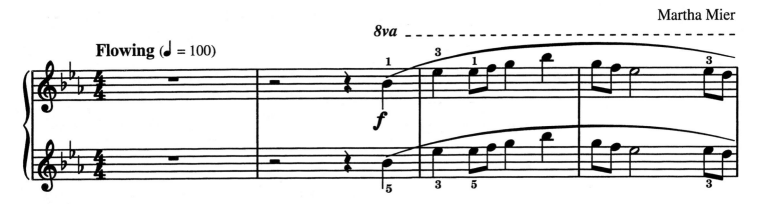

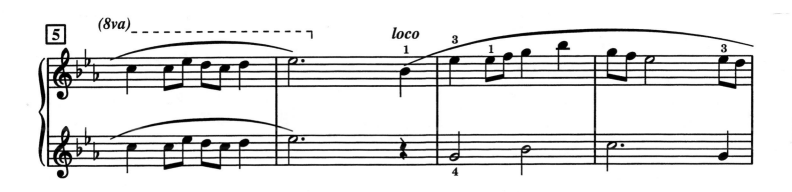

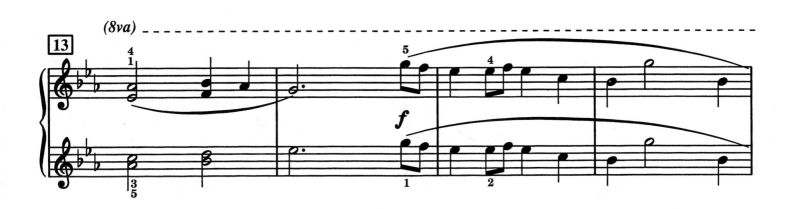

Secondo

Primo

Spanish Gypsies

Secondo

Martha Mier

Spanish Gypsies

Primo

Martha Mier

Secondo

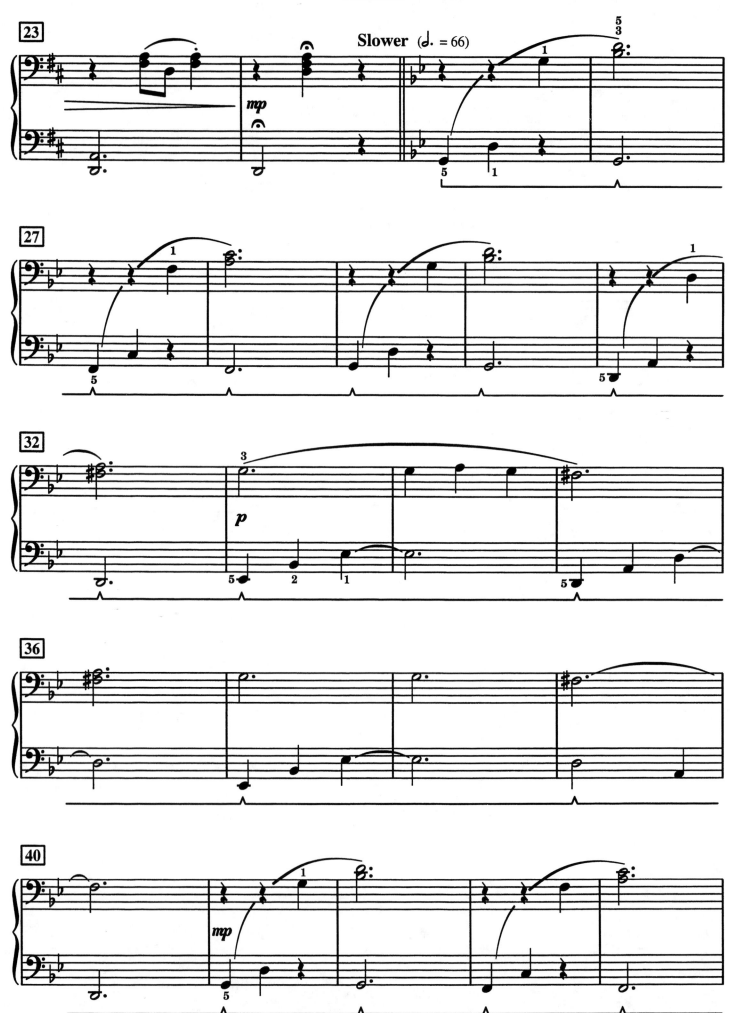

Primo

Secondo

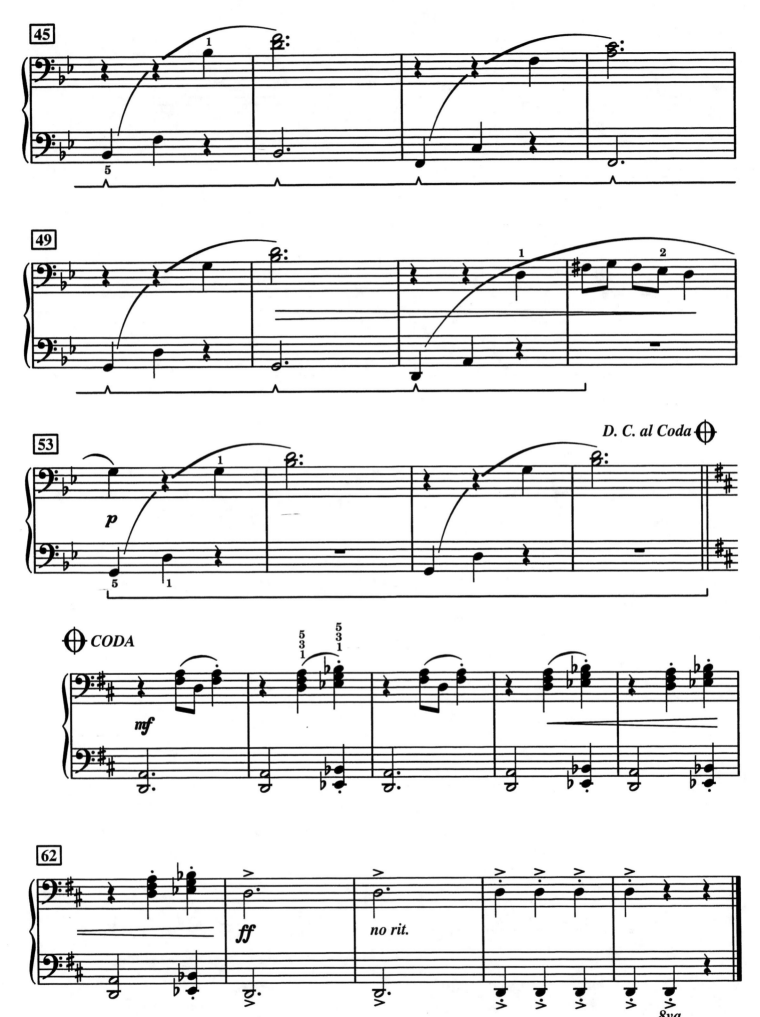

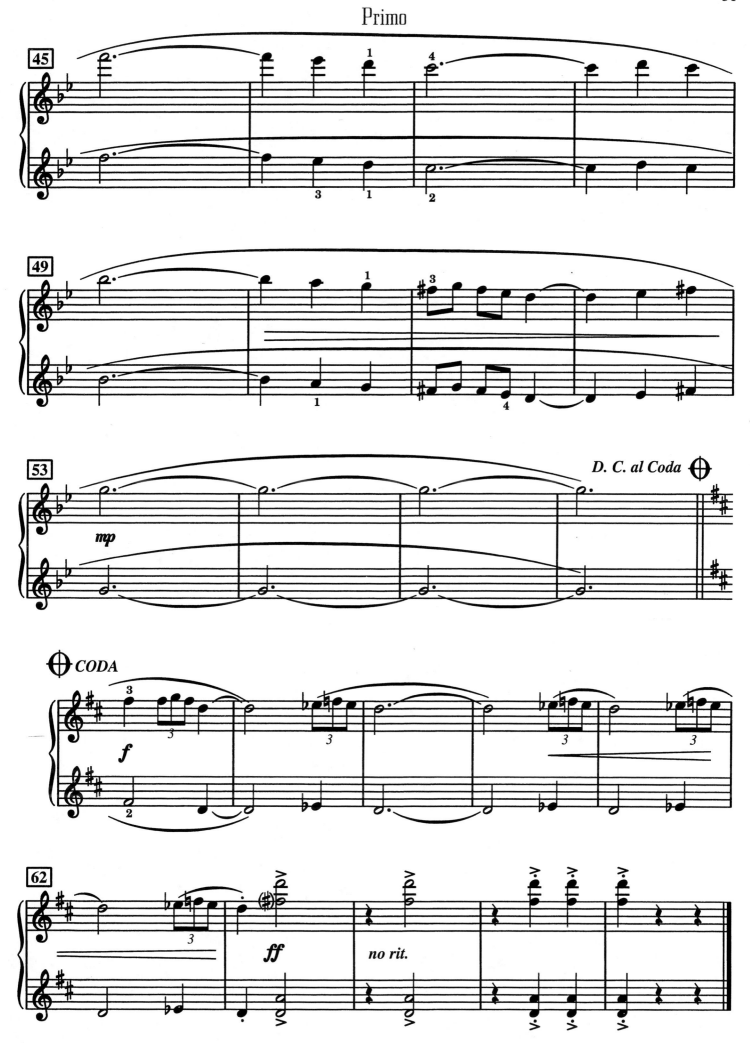

Primo